Piano

*for Keisuke Wakao*

# THE DAYS BETWEEN

From the Columbia Pictures film STEPMOM

For Solo Oboe and Piano

## JOHN WILLIAMS

ISBN 0-634-00766-1

Visit Hal Leonard Online at
**www.halleonard.com**

HAL•LEONARD®
CORPORATION

7777 W. BLUEMOUND RD. P.O. BOX 13819 MILWAUKEE, WI 53213

*for Keisuke Wakao*

# THE DAYS BETWEEN

From the Columbia Pictures film STEPMOM

JOHN WILLIAMS

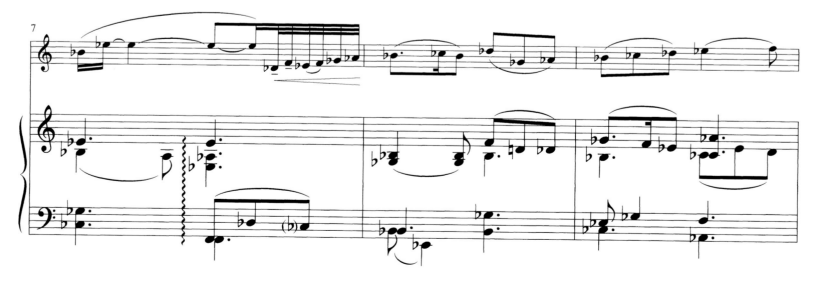

**Poco mouvt.**

Solo Oboe

*for Keisuke Wakao*

# THE DAYS BETWEEN

From the Columbia Pictures film STEPMOM

For Solo Oboe and Piano

## JOHN WILLIAMS

ISBN 0-634-00766-1

Visit Hal Leonard Online at
**www.halleonard.com**

7777 W. BLUEMOUND RD. P.O. BOX 13819 MILWAUKEE, WI 53213

*for Keisuke Wakao*
# THE DAYS BETWEEN
From the Columbia Pictures film STEPMOM

JOHN WILLIAMS

**OBOE**

**Moderato (in 6)**
*"Alla Siciliana"*

**Poco mouvt.**

**43** **Move a little**

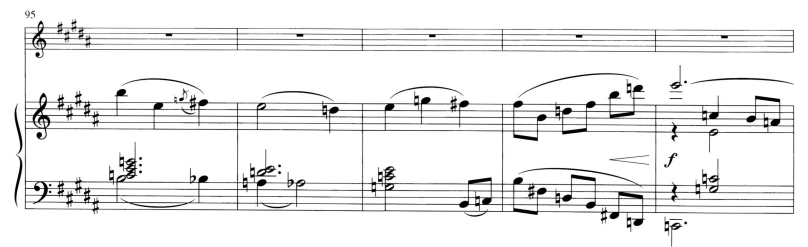

**Slightly Slower**

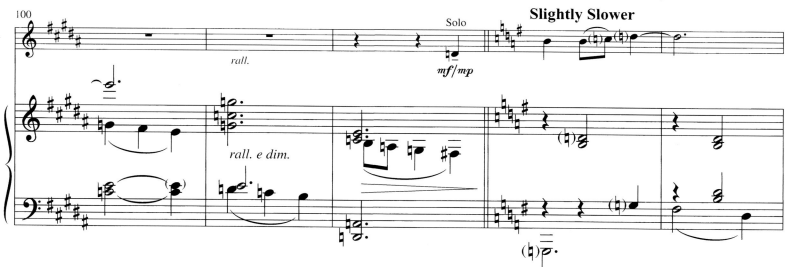

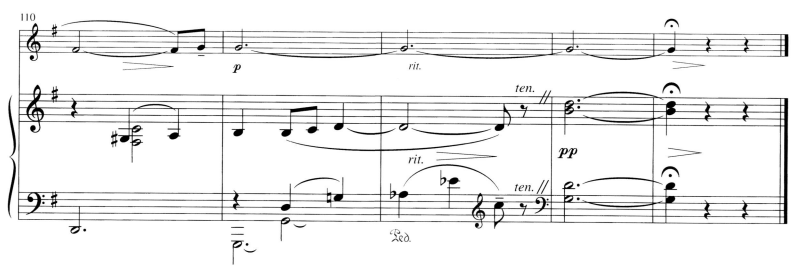